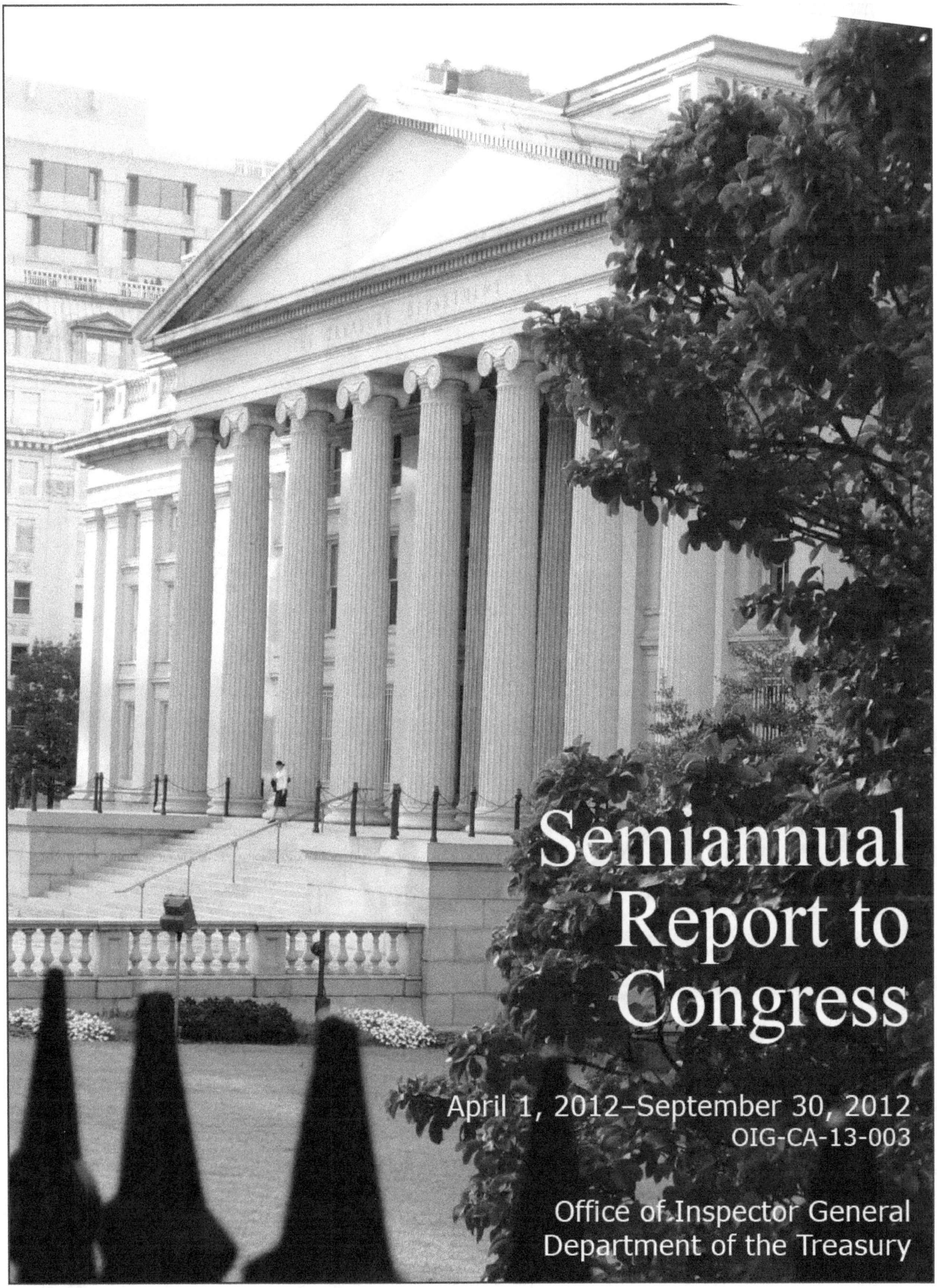

Semiannual Report to Congress

April 1, 2012–September 30, 2012
OIG-CA-13-003

Office of Inspector General
Department of the Treasury

Highlights

During this semiannual reporting period, our Office of Audit issued 33 products and our Office of Small Business Lending Fund Program Oversight issued 4. Work by our Office of Investigations resulted in 12 arrests and 15 convictions. Some of our more significant results for the period are described below.

- We audited Treasury's role in the $535 million loan guarantee made to Solyndra in 2009. We found Treasury performed a consultation on the terms and conditions of the Solyndra loan guarantee as derived from law and regulation implementing the Department of Energy's Loan Guarantee Program. However, whether that consultation met the intent of the applicable law and regulation is not clear because Treasury's consultative role was not sufficiently defined. The consultation that did occur was rushed, and no documentation was retained as to how Treasury's serious concerns with the loan guarantee were addressed.

- We reported that the Office of the Comptroller of the Currency's examination procedures during the period 2008 through 2010 were not sufficient in scope or application to identify significant weaknesses in national banks' foreclosure documentation and processing functions. The office did not consider foreclosure documentation and processing to be an area of significant risk and, as a result, did not focus examination resources on this function.

- Our Office of Small Business Lending Fund Program Oversight reported that most of the $3.6 million spent by California for the State Small Business Credit Initiative was used properly. However, $133,000 in loan loss reserves funded under California's Small Business Loan Guarantee Program did not meet requirements. The expenditures constituted a "reckless" misuse of funds, which under the Small Business Jobs Act, Treasury must recoup. California also reported $161,000 in administrative expenses that appeared reasonable but were not supported by proper documentation.

- With respect to the $30 billion Small Business Lending Fund, we determined that 8 out of 10 institutions we sampled incorrectly reported qualified lending gains associated with their small business lending activity. The institutions' errors totaled $74 million, most of which was attributed to one bank over-reporting its baseline by $48 million, or 43 percent.

- We investigated a senior official based on an allegation of time and attendance fraud and determined the official owed the Bureau of the Public Debt over 1,200 hours between 2009 to 2012, or approximately $97,800 in salary. The case was referred to bureau management for administrative action.

- A former bank president was sentenced in the U.S. District Court in Aberdeen, Mississippi, to 63 months of imprisonment and ordered to pay a $100 special assessment and $1.5 million in restitution for diverting funds to pay personal bills. The former bank president also subverted the Office of the Comptroller of the Currency's examination process by concealing the true identity of borrowers on several loans and concealing the condition of the loans which led to the failure of First National Bank of Rosedale.

Message From the Inspector General

I am pleased to provide our Semiannual Report for the 6 months ending September 30, 2012. As our mandated work related to bank failures has decreased, we have been able to redirect resources to audit work in Treasury's activities intended to support economic recovery as well as audit work designed to address areas of current and emerging risks as they related to Treasury programs and operations.

For example, we reviewed Treasury's consultative role regarding the $535 million loan guarantee made to Solyndra, where we found that Treasury did consult on the loan as was required by law. However, we also found that Treasury's consultative role was poorly defined and that important issues seemed to be unresolved at the time the loan guarantee was approved. Accordingly, we recommended that Treasury work with the Department of Energy to clearly define what is expected in Treasury's consultation and provide Treasury adequate time to carry out its consultative processes.

Other notable audit work includes 5 audit reports related to oversight of Treasury's spending authority under the Recovery Act. We also, at the request of the Chairman of the Senate Committee on Banking, Housing and Urban Affairs, reviewed the Office of the Comptroller of the Currency's community bank examination and appeals process. Additionally, we responded to an inquiry by the Ranking Member of the Senate Finance Committee on the debt limit crisis of July and August 2011.

Our Office of Small Business Lending Fund Program Oversight completed two reviews addressing the soundness of early investment decisions and the calculation of the program's initial dividend rate. We found that 80 percent of the institutions sampled incorrectly reported qualified lending gains. As a result, the Treasury's October 26, 2011, *Use of Funds* report, over-reported lending increases for some institutions and under-reported for others. If not corrected, these errors will continue in subsequent reports. I noted in previous Semiannual Reports that the Office of Small Business Lending Fund Program Oversight was auditing the use of federal funds provided to states by the $1.5 billion State Small Business Credit Initiative to support lending to small businesses. Our reviews have identified misused funds that Treasury must recoup and recommended the disallowance of administrative expenses that were not properly supported.

The Council of Inspectors General on Financial Oversight (CIGFO), which I chair, convened its first working group under the leadership of the Federal Deposit Insurance Corporation's Inspector General, Jon Rymer. I am pleased to note that the working group issued its report, *Audit of the Financial Stability Oversight Council's Controls over Non-public Information*, in June of this year. The report identified differences in how the federal agency members of the Financial Stability Oversight Council, and the Council itself, control non-public information. The CIGFO report acknowledged that the Financial Stability Oversight Council is evolving and some information-sharing projects are under development. CIGFO encouraged the Council to further examine the issues raised in the report.

The Office of Investigations continues to transition to significant criminal, civil, and administrative cases that pose risk of fraud, waste, and abuse in the Department's programs and operations. Our investigations have led to a number of prosecutions, convictions, and restitutions. Recent investigative work ranged from cases involving embezzlement, theft, and tax evasion, to seizure of millions of dollars of mutilated currency. Collaborative efforts by our investigators with other agencies have resulted in, for example, a former bank president pleading guilty to embezzlement; the sentencing in this case included over $1.5 million in restitution. Another collaboration involved embezzlement from TreasuryDirect accounts and Orange County, Florida, businesses.

At the suggestion of Senator Tester, and encouraged by the example of the Department of Justice Office of Inspector General, my office took steps to implement a Whistleblower Ombudsman Initiative, by which Treasury employees will have a central point of contact within the office to learn of their rights and obligations under the Whistleblower Protection Act. This initiative will enable my office to better coordinate with the Office of Special Counsel. We now plan to engage in outreach to Treasury bureaus and offices.

At the request of Chairwoman Emerson of the Financial Services and General Government Subcommittee of the House Committee on Appropriations, we conducted an inquiry regarding the Department's July 16, 2012, website posting entitled "Penny Wise and Pound Foolish," where the Department expressed its views on funding levels for two non-Treasury agencies, the Securities and Exchange Commission and the Commodity Futures Trading Commission. Ms. Emerson asked us to look at whether the Department's outreach may have violated statutory prohibitions and limitations on using appropriated funds to lobby Congress and otherwise advocate for legislative action. We reviewed the statutory provisions, as well as analyses and interpretations of them, and interviewed Departmental officials with knowledge of and responsibility for the posting, and adherence to the legal constraints. We concluded that the outreach at issue did not violate the applicable law. Additionally, we determined that there is a legal review process in place to ensure that public outreach efforts do not violate the anti-lobbying laws.

In closing, I would like to express my appreciation for the continued support and responsiveness of Treasury's senior leadership to our oversight findings and recommendations. I would also like to acknowledge the employees of Treasury's Office of Inspector General for their diligence, dedication, and professionalism. They are integral in helping Treasury meet its mission.

Eric M. Thorson
Inspector General

Contents

Office of Inspector General Overview

The Department of the Treasury's Office of Inspector General (OIG) was established pursuant to the 1988 amendments to the Inspector General Act of 1978. OIG is headed by an Inspector General appointed by the President, with the advice and consent of the Senate.

OIG performs independent, objective reviews of Treasury programs and operations, except for those of the Internal Revenue Service (IRS) and the Troubled Asset Relief Program (TARP), and keeps the Secretary of the Treasury and Congress fully informed of problems, deficiencies, and the need for corrective action. The Treasury Inspector General for Tax Administration performs oversight related to IRS. A Special Inspector General and the Government Accountability Office perform oversight related to TARP.

OIG has five components: (1) Office of Audit, (2) Office of Investigations, (3) Office of Small Business Lending Fund (SBLF) Program Oversight, (4) Office of Counsel, and (5) Office of Management. OIG is headquartered in Washington, D.C., and has an audit office in Boston, Massachusetts.

The Office of Audit, under the leadership of the Assistant Inspector General for Audit, performs and supervises audits, attestation engagements, and evaluations. The Assistant Inspector General for Audit has two deputies. One is primarily responsible for performance audits, and the other is primarily responsible for financial management, information technology (IT), and financial assistance audits.

The Office of Investigations, under the leadership of the Assistant Inspector General for Investigations, performs investigations and conducts initiatives to detect and prevent fraud, waste, and abuse in Treasury programs and operations under our jurisdiction. It also manages the Treasury OIG Hotline to facilitate reporting of allegations involving Treasury programs and activities.

The Office of SBLF Program Oversight, under the leadership of a Special Deputy Inspector General, conducts, supervises, and coordinates audits and investigations of SBLF and the State Small Business Credit Initiative (SSBCI).

The Office of Counsel, under the leadership of the Counsel to the Inspector General, provides legal advice to the Inspector General and all OIG components. The office represents the OIG in administrative legal proceedings and provides a variety of legal services including (1) processing Freedom of Information Act and *Giglio* requests; (2) conducting ethics training; (3) ensuring compliance with financial disclosure requirements; (4) reviewing proposed legislation and regulations; (5) reviewing administrative subpoena requests; and (6) preparing for the Inspector General's signature, cease and desist letters to be sent to persons and entities misusing the Treasury seal and name.

The Office of Management, under the leadership of the Assistant Inspector General for Management, provides services to maintain the OIG administrative infrastructure.

As of September 30, 2012, OIG had 173 full-time staff. Fifteen of those staff work for the Office of SBLF Program Oversight and are funded on a reimbursable basis. OIG's fiscal year 2012 appropriation is $29.6 million.

Treasury's Management and Performance Challenges

In accordance with the Reports Consolidation Act of 2000, the Treasury Inspector General annually provides the Secretary of the Treasury with our perspective on the most serious management and performance challenges facing the Department of the Treasury. In a memorandum to Secretary Geithner dated October 25, 2012, Inspector General Thorson reported one new challenge—Gulf Coast Restoration Trust Fund Administration—and three challenges from last year. One previously reported challenge was removed. The following is an abridged version of that memorandum.

Transformation of Financial Regulation (Repeat Challenge)

The Dodd-Frank Wall Street Reform and Consumer Protection Act (Dodd-Frank) established new responsibilities for Treasury and created new offices tasked to fulfill those responsibilities.

For example, Dodd-Frank established the Financial Stability Oversight Council (FSOC), chaired by the Secretary of the Treasury, whose mission is to identify risks to financial stability that could arise from the activities of large, interconnected financial companies; respond to any emerging threats to the financial system; and promote market discipline. FSOC accomplished a number of things over the past year. As required, FSOC also issued its second annual report. The report contained recommendations to (1) further reforms to address structural vulnerabilities in key markets, (2) heighten risk management and supervisory attention in specific areas, (3) take steps to address reform of the housing finance market, and (4) ensure implementation and coordination on financial regulatory reform. FSOC also designated eight financial market utilities as systemically important. That said, FSOC still has work ahead to meet all of its responsibilities. For example, it remains in the process of designating the first group of nonbank financial institutions for consolidated supervision.

The Council of Inspectors General on Financial Oversight (CIGFO), chaired by the Treasury Inspector General, also established by Dodd-Frank, is an important source of independent analysis to FSOC. Among its activities, CIGFO established its first working group to evaluate FSOC controls over non-public information and the manner in which FSOC, as a whole, safeguarded information from unauthorized sources. The resulting report highlighted several areas for FSOC's consideration. CIGFO will continue reviewing FSOC's compliance with the requirements of Dodd-Frank.

Dodd-Frank also established two new offices within Treasury: the Office of Financial Research (OFR) and the Federal Insurance Office (FIO). OFR is the data collection, research and analysis arm of FSOC. We completed a review of the stand-up of OFR and reported that in the 21 months since OFR was created, efforts to establish the office were still in progress. FIO is charged with monitoring the insurance industry. We are currently reviewing the stand-up of FIO.

The other regulatory challenges that we discussed last year remain. Specifically, since September 2007, 126 Treasury-regulated financial institutions have failed, with estimated losses to the Deposit Insurance Fund (DIF) of approximately $35.3 billion. With more than 450 banks on the Federal Deposit Insurance

Corporation's (FDIC) troubled bank list, we anticipate bank failures to continue into the foreseeable future but at a lower rate than in recent years.

Clearly, as we have said in the past, the intention of Dodd-Frank is most notably to prevent, or at least minimize, the impact of a future financial sector crisis on the U.S. economy. This management challenge from our perspective is to maintain an effective FSOC process and build a streamlined banking regulatory structure that timely identifies and strongly responds to emerging risks.

Management of Treasury's Authorities Intended to Support and Improve the Economy (Repeat Challenge)

Congress provided Treasury with broad authorities to address the recent financial crisis under the Housing and Economic Recovery Act (HERA) and the Emergency Economic Stabilization Act (EESA), the American Recovery and Reinvestment Act (Recovery Act), and the Small Business Jobs Act. Although challenges remain, Treasury's program administration under HERA, EESA, and the Recovery Act has matured. However, the long-term impact on small business lending resulting from investment decisions under the Small Business Jobs Act programs are not yet entirely clear.

SBLF and SSBCI

The Small Business Jobs Act created the $30 billion SBLF within Treasury and provided $1.5 billion to Treasury to allocate to eligible state programs through SSBCI. As of September 2011, Treasury disbursed more than $4 billion to 332 financial institutions across the

country. Institutions receiving investments under the SBLF program pay dividends to Treasury at rates that decrease as the institutions increase their qualified lending activity. Treasury faces challenges in measuring program performance and ensuring that the SBLF program meets its intended objective of increasing lending to small businesses. As of September 2012, 56 states, territories, and eligible municipalities had been awarded $1.4 billion in SSBCI funding. Funds awarded are disbursed in one-third increments. To date, Treasury disbursed $533 million of the award. We audit participating states to determine whether SSBCI funds are being used as intended. In this regard, Treasury is required to recoup funds we identify as having been recklessly or intentionally misused, and Treasury may withhold disbursements from a state based on the audit results. We noted several challenges facing Treasury in holding states accountable for the proper use of funds.

Recovery Act Programs

Treasury is responsible for overseeing an estimated $150 billion of Recovery Act funding and tax relief. Treasury's oversight responsibilities include programs that provide payments for specified energy property in lieu of tax credits, payments to states for low-income housing projects in lieu of tax credits, and grants and tax credits through the Community Development Financial Institutions (CDFI) Fund. About $20 billion of the $22 billion provided for non-IRS programs has been disbursed to recipients under Treasury's payments in lieu of tax credit programs. To date, all funds have been disbursed under the low-income housing program and the specified energy property program is winding down. Treasury must continue to ensure recipient compliance with award agreements going forward.

HERA and EESA

Under HERA, Treasury continued to support the financial solvency of the Federal National Mortgage Association (Fannie Mae) and the Federal Home Loan Mortgage Corporation (Freddie Mac) which are under the conservatorship of the Federal Housing Finance Agency. As of June 2012, Treasury invested a total of $187 billion in the two entities to cover their losses and maintain a positive net worth. Although Fannie Mae and Freddie Mac reported a positive net worth in the first and second quarters of 2012, the future of both entities is still in question and prolonged assistance may be required.

TARP, established by EESA, gave Treasury authorities necessary to bolster credit availability and address other serious problems in the domestic and world financial markets. Through several of the TARP programs, Treasury made purchases of direct loans and equity investments in many financial institutions and other businesses, as well as guaranteed other troubled mortgage-related and financial assets. One Treasury challenge in this area is managing and winding down its various investment programs.

Anti-Money Laundering and Terrorist Financing/Bank Secrecy Act Enforcement (Repeat Challenge)

Ensuring criminals and terrorists do not use our financial networks to sustain their operations and/or launch attacks against the U.S. continues to be a challenge. Treasury's Office of Terrorism and Financial Intelligence is dedicated to disrupting the ability of terrorist

organizations to fund their operations. This office brings together intelligence gathering and analysis, economic sanctions, international cooperation, and private-sector cooperation to identify donors, financiers, and facilitators supporting terrorist organizations, and disrupt their ability to fund them. Enhancing the transparency of the financial system is one of the cornerstones of this effort. Treasury carries out its responsibilities to enhance financial transparency through the Bank Secrecy Act (BSA) and USA Patriot Act. The Financial Crimes Enforcement Network (FinCEN) is responsible for administering BSA.

Over the past decade, the Office of Terrorism and Financial Intelligence has made progress in addressing vulnerabilities that allowed money launderers and terrorists to use the financial system to support their activities. Nonetheless, significant challenges remain. One challenge is ensuring the continued cooperation and coordination among the entities involved in anti-money laundering and combating terrorist financing efforts. Many of these entities also participate in efforts to ensure compliance with U.S. foreign sanction programs administered by Treasury's Office of Foreign Assets Control (OFAC). To be effective, Treasury must establish and maintain working relationships with these numerous entities.

Last year, financial institutions filed approximately 17 million BSA reports, including over 1.5 million suspicious activity reports. While the number of suspicious activity reports has been increasing since 2001, the numbers alone do not necessarily indicate everything is going well. Audits we have done have found problems with the quality of the data reported. Other audits have also identified gaps in the regulatory examination programs of the bank regulators and examining agencies. FinCEN needs to continue its efforts to work with regulators and examining agencies to ensure that financial institutions establish effective BSA compliance programs and file accurate and complete BSA reports, as required. Furthermore, FinCEN needs to complete work to issue anti-money laundering regulations as it determines appropriate for some non-bank financial institutions, such as vehicle dealers; pawnbrokers; travel agents; finance companies; real estate closing and settlement services; and financial services intermediaries, such as investment advisors.

We noted that FinCEN has a particularly difficult challenge in dealing with money service businesses. To that end, FinCEN has taken steps to improve money service business examination coverage and compliance. However, ensuring money service businesses register with FinCEN has been a challenge. Furthermore, IRS serves as the examining agency, but has limited resources to inspect or even identify unregistered money service businesses.

Other matters of concern include one that we reported on previously. It is that the focus on safety and soundness resulting from the recent financial crisis may have reduced the attention financial institutions are giving to BSA and OFAC compliance. Another concern is the increasing use of mobile devices for banking, internet banking, internet gaming, and peer-to-peer transactions. FinCEN, OFAC, and other regulatory agencies will need to ensure that providers of these services ensure transactions are transparent and conform to BSA requirements.

Given the criticality of this management challenge to the Department's mission, we continue to consider anti-money laundering and combating terrorist financing as inherently high-risk.

Gulf Coast Restoration Trust Fund Administration

In response to the Deepwater Horizon oil spill, Congress established within Treasury the Gulf Coast Restoration Trust Fund and requires Treasury to deposit in the Trust Fund 80 percent of administrative and civil penalties paid by responsible parties for the Deepwater Horizon oil spill. It is estimated that the Trust Fund could receive tens of billions of dollars from these penalties to be distributed for eligible activities affecting the Gulf Coast states (Alabama, Florida, Louisiana, Mississippi, and Texas). Treasury, in consultation with the Departments of the Interior and Commerce, is required to develop policies and procedures to administer the Trust Fund by early January 2013. Congress also authorized our office to conduct, supervise, and coordinate audits and investigations of projects, programs and activities funded under this legislation. Neither Treasury nor our office was provided funding in the act for carrying out our respective responsibilities.

What makes the administration of the Trust Fund so challenging is that (1) regulations and associated policies and procedures need to be established and put into place quickly; (2) many of the entities/councils that are to receive and further allocate funding were not created before the enactment of the legislation and need to establish their own policies and procedures; and (3) there are many entities/councils that must cooperate for the funds to be distributed and spent in an appropriate manner. Also, as noted, Treasury must use existing resources to administer its responsibilities.

Other Information Provided

In past memorandums, we included Management of Capital Investments on the list of the most serious management and performance challenges. In this regard, we had reported on a number of capital investment projects that either failed or had serious problems. However, we believe Treasury's implementation activities for two capital investments, Treasury Network (TNet) and FinCEN's BSA IT Modernization (BSA IT Mod) program, while not perfect, demonstrated that the Department has made sufficient, sustainable improvement in managing and mitigating investment risk to warrant removal of this area from the list this year.

Our memorandum also highlighted three areas of concern with cyber security, challenges with currency and coin production, and lapses by the Department in maintaining a complete and concurrent record of key activities and decisions.

We further noted that in October 2012, the Department undertook a consolidation and restructuring of the Bureau of the Public Debt (BPD) and Financial Management Service (FMS) into the Bureau of the Fiscal Service. Expected to save substantial dollars in the long run, the initiative is laudable. Furthermore, early indications are that planning for the consolidation, as well as communication with affected personnel, has been extensive. However, we made the observation such that consolidations do entail risk as separate processes, systems, and workplace cultures are meshed together.

The Inspector General's annual Management and Performance Challenges Memoranda are available on the Treasury OIG website.

Office of Audit – Significant Audits and Other Products

Products Supporting the Council of Inspectors General on Financial Oversight

Audit of the Financial Stability Oversight Council's Controls over Non-public Information

Dodd-Frank created, among other things, the CIGFO. One of CIGFO's statutory functions is to provide oversight of the FSOC. Specifically, the law grants CIGFO the authority to convene a working group, by a majority vote, for the purpose of evaluating the effectiveness and internal operations of FSOC. During fiscal year 2012, CIGFO convened a working group led by the FDIC Inspector General to examine FSOC's controls and protocols for ensuring that its non-public information, deliberations, and decisions are properly safeguarded from unauthorized disclosure. Participating in the working group were the OIGs of FDIC, Board of Governors of the Federal Reserve System (FRB) and Consumer Financial Protection Bureau, Commodity Futures Trading Commission, Treasury, Federal Housing Finance Agency, National Credit Union Administration, and Securities and Exchange Commission. Work was conducted at OFR, FIO, and the Office of the Comptroller of the Currency (OCC).

FSOC acknowledges that its ability to safely share information among its members is critical to its effectiveness. To date, a limited amount of non-public information has been exchanged among FSOC members. Collaborations among FSOC members to identify and mitigate risks to financial stability has begun, and the data sharing will expand as OFR continues to build its capacity. To protect the exchange of information, FSOC members entered into a memorandum of understanding governing the treatment of non-public information that relies on each agency to use the controls in place at their respective agencies. The working group identified differences in how FSOC agency members mark non-public information as well as differences for handling non-public information. Without addressing these differences, there is a risk that senders and receivers of FSOC non-public information may not apply a consistent level of controls.

In its June 2012 report, the working group acknowledged that FSOC is still evolving and a number of information-sharing projects are under development. For this reason, the working group has not made any recommendations, for now. However, the working group encouraged FSOC to continue its ongoing efforts, to further examine the issues raised in the report with respect to commonalities and differences of member agencies, and to prepare for possible security upgrades for information that may need to be exchanged as economic conditions change and new threats to the stability of the U.S. financial system emerge.

Response to a Congressional Inquiry Related to Raising the Debt Limit

We responded to an October 2011 and January 2012 inquiry by the Ranking Member of the Senate Finance Committee on the debt limit crisis of late July/early August 2011. In that inquiry, the Ranking Member asked CIGFO to review FSOC's responses to inquiries that he made regarding the debt limit. More specifically, the inquiry related to (1) Treasury's cash projections during July and August, (2) contingency plans developed by FSOC voting member agencies if the debt limit had not been raised or if there was a credit rating downgrade on the U.S., (3) FSOC's compliance with statutory requirements for identifying risks and responding to emerging threats to financial stability, and (4) FSOC's reporting on systemic risks surrounding the debt limit. As this was determined to be primarily a Treasury issue, we performed the work and prepared the response.

We reviewed Treasury's daily cash balance projections as of July 21, 2011, for the period July 28 to August 31, 2011. We noted that absent an increase to the debt limit, our analysis of these projections showed that a sufficient cash balance would not be available to meet all incoming due obligations by August 11, 2011. Furthermore, the cash deficit would grow with each day that the debt limit was not raised.

We also determined that FSOC met its statutory requirements under Dodd-Frank to identify, respond, and report on systemic risks and emerging threats to the U.S. financial system. According to the Treasury's Deputy Assistant Secretary for the FSOC, individual FSOC members recognized the fiscal policy challenge, but there was no collective initiative by FSOC to create an FSOC-directed and coordinated set of contingency plans had the debt limit not been raised. **(OIG-CA-12-006)**

Treasury Has Made Progress to Stand-up OFR

Given the criticality of OFR to FSOC's mission, we initiated an audit to evaluate the effectiveness and status of Treasury's process to establish OFR. We reported that as of April 2012, 21 months after OFR was created, efforts to establish the office were still in progress. The officials responsible for establishing the office initially engaged in high-level strategic and organizational planning and sought to hire key personnel. They also focused on developing and facilitating the global acceptance of a universal Legal Entity Identifier,[1] while leveraging Treasury's Departmental Offices to support administrative functions. In the summer of 2011, after key operational personnel were brought on board, progress toward establishing a comprehensive implementation planning and project management process accelerated. This culminated in the approval of OFR's Project Management Methodology in January 2012, OFR's Strategic Framework in March 2012, and OFR's Strategic Roadmap in April 2012. While not finalized until well over a year after it was established, these documents and methodology, taken together, now provide OFR with a comprehensive implementation plan. This plan lays out the expected evolution of the office's capabilities, reaching a mature state by fiscal year 2016.

Concurrent with the development of its comprehensive implementation plan, OFR also began to develop its analytic and data support for FSOC. Its Research and Analysis Center has sponsored seminars and published two working papers on risk assessment topics.

We recommended that OFR monitor its progress in carrying out the activities in the comprehensive implementation plan and take actions timely to address any slippages or otherwise make adjustments so as to achieve the

---

[1] Legal Entity Identifier is being developed as the universal standard for identifying all parties to financial contracts. It is a key element in OFR's effort to understand and monitor risks to financial stability and meet its statutory mandate to develop and promote data standards.

objectives and timeframes in the plan. The office's planned corrective action was responsive to our recommendation. **(OIG-12-057)**

Performance Audits of Treasury Programs and Operations

Consultation on Solyndra Loan Guarantee Was Rushed

Due to heightened media attention and congressional inquiry surrounding the bankruptcy of Solyndra LLC (Solyndra), we initiated an audit of Treasury's role in the $535 million loan guarantee made to the company in 2009. This loan was 100 percent guaranteed by the Department of Energy and funded by Treasury's Federal Financing Bank. Our audit objectives were to (1) determine Treasury's responsibilities related to the Department of Energy's loan guarantee for Solyndra as established by applicable laws, regulations, policies, procedures, and agreements and (2) assess whether Treasury appropriately carried out those responsibilities.

Treasury 's consultative role as it related to the Solyndra loan guarantee is derived from (1) Title XVII of the Energy Policy Act of 2005, as amended by the Recovery Act; (2) the Federal Financing Bank Act; and (3) 10 CFR §609 (Final Rule implementing Title XVII of the Act).

We found that Treasury did perform a consultation on the terms and conditions of the Solyndra loan guarantee. However, whether that consultation met the intent of the applicable law and regulation is not clear because Treasury's consultative role was not sufficiently defined. The consultation that did occur was rushed, and

no documentation was retained as to how Treasury's serious concerns with the loan were addressed.

Treasury management generally agreed with our recommendations to (1) work with the Department of Energy to establish a definition of what Treasury's consultative role is and what it should include; (2) work with the Department of Energy to establish a common understanding of what would be considered a deviation that constitutes a substantial change in the financial terms and conditions of a loan guarantee and require Treasury's consultation; and (3) develop and implement written policies and procedures to govern Treasury's consultative process. However, Treasury did not agree with a statement in our report that Treasury's consultation should broadly reflect *"…its perspective on the amount to be guaranteed, reasonable prospect of repayment, interest rate, remedies for default, fees charged to the applicant, and the full faith and credit pledge of the United States."* In this regard, Treasury believes that some of these matters relate to an applicant's creditworthiness which is an issue that Congress placed solely within the Department of Energy's purview under the Act, and that Treasury's input is limited to the interest rate and other terms and conditions of the potential loan guarantee. In our evaluation of Treasury's response, however, we noted that as provided in section 1702 of the Act, the Secretary of the Treasury provides consultation on a number of terms and conditions, such as the specific appropriation or contribution, amount, repayment, interest rate, term, defaults, fees, records and audits, and full faith and credit. **(OIG-12-048)**

Failed Bank Reviews

In 1991, Congress enacted the Federal Deposit Insurance Corporation Improvement Act following the failures of about a thousand banks and thrifts from 1986 to 1990. Among other things, the act added Section 38, Prompt

Corrective Action, to the Federal Deposit Insurance Act (FDIA). Section 38 requires federal banking agencies to take specific supervisory actions in response to certain circumstances.[2]

Section 38 also requires the Inspector General for the primary federal regulator[3] of a failed financial institution to conduct a material loss review (MLR) when the estimated loss to the DIF is "material." An MLR requires that we determine the causes of the failure and assess the supervision of the institution, including the implementation of the Section 38 Prompt Corrective Action provisions. Section 38, as amended by Dodd-Frank, defines a material loss as a loss to the DIF that exceeds $150 million for 2012 and 2013, and $50 million in 2014 and thereafter, with a provision for increasing the threshold to $75 million under certain circumstances. Section 38 also requires a review of all bank failures with losses under those threshold amounts for the purposes of (1) ascertaining the grounds identified by OCC for appointing FDIC as receiver, and (2) determining whether any unusual circumstances exist that might warrant a more in-depth review of the loss. This provision

applies to bank failures from October 1, 2009, forward.[4]

From the beginning of the recent economic crisis in 2007 through September 2012, FDIC and other banking regulators closed 458 banks and thrifts. Treasury, through OCC and the former Office of Thrift Supervision (OTS), was responsible for regulating 126 of those institutions. Of the 126 failures, 54 resulted in a material loss to the DIF. There were no new failures of Treasury-regulated banks that required an MLR during this semiannual reporting period. During this period, we completed 1 MLR from the prior reporting period and 1 in-depth review. Since 2007, we have completed 54 MLRs and 3 in-depth reviews.

As previously reported, from the MLRs we have completed, we have seen a number of trends emerge. With respect to the causes of these institutions' failures, we found significant losses in loan portfolios, poor underwriting and overly aggressive growth strategies fueled by volatile and costly wholesale funding (e.g., brokered deposits, Federal Home Loan Bank loans); risky lending products such as option adjustable rate mortgages; high asset concentrations; and inadequate risk management systems. In addition, the management and boards of these institutions were often ineffective. The economic recession and the decline in the real estate market were also factors in most of the failures.

---

[2] Prompt corrective action is a framework of supervisory actions for insured institutions that are not adequately capitalized. It was intended to ensure that action is taken when an institution becomes financially troubled in order to prevent a failure or minimize resulting losses. These actions become increasingly more severe as the institution falls into lower capital categories. The capital categories are well-capitalized, adequately capitalized, undercapitalized, significantly undercapitalized, and critically undercapitalized.

[3] Within Treasury, OCC is the regulator for national banks. Effective July 21, 2011, OCC assumed the regulatory responsibility for federal savings associations that were previously regulated by the former Office of Thrift Supervision.

---

[4] Prior to Dodd-Frank, an MLR was required if loss to the DIF from a bank failure exceeded the greater of $25 million or 2 percent of the institution's total assets. There was also no requirement for us to review bank failures with losses less than this threshold.

With respect to OCC's and the former OTS's oversight, we found that both regulators conducted regular and timely examinations and identified operational problems, but were slow to take timely and effective enforcement actions. We also found that in assessing these institutions, examiners regularly gave too much weight to profitability and performing loans and not enough to the amount of risk these institutions had taken on. We also noted that regulators took appropriate prompt corrective actions when warranted but those actions did not prevent a material loss to the DIF.

Material Loss and In-Depth Reviews

Material Loss Review of Integra Bank (closed July 29, 2011; estimated loss to the DIF - $205.9 million)

Our MLR found that Integra Bank (Integra), Evansville, Indiana, failed because it pursued an aggressive growth strategy which led to high concentrations in commercial real estate loans. In connection with its strategy, Integra paid a significant premium to acquire Prairie Bank and Trust Company, a state chartered bank in the Chicago metropolitan area with weak credit administration processes and a commercial real estate loan portfolio of inferior asset quality With the economic downturn, the performance of Integra's commercial real estate loans declined. This decline in performance led to sustained loan losses and required Integra to write off its entire goodwill balance, including goodwill that was recorded when it acquired the trust company.

We determined that OCC provided ongoing supervision of Integra through regular on-site and off-site reviews. Although OCC's supervision did not prevent a material loss to the insurance fund, we concluded that its

supervision of Integra was appropriate. In addition, we concluded that OCC appropriately implemented prompt corrective actions as the bank's capital levels fell.

We also reported on three other matters regarding OCC's supervision of Integra. Specifically, (1) OCC's examination working papers for Integra were not complete, a deficiency we have noted in prior material loss reviews; (2) OCC examiners reviewed Integra's due diligence performed in connection with the Prairie Bank and Trust Company acquisition, however, OCC does not have formal guidance for examiners to use when evaluating bank acquisitions; and (3) with regard to OCC's review process for recommending approval of the TARP application by Integra's holding company, certain information about Integra's financial condition, such as a potential goodwill impairment, was not included in the OCC TARP case decision memo.

In addition to the estimated loss to the DIF, FDIC estimated that the failure of Integra would result in a loss of $51 million to FDIC's Debt Guarantee Program. Also, Treasury expects that the $83.6 million that was provided to Integra's holding company under TARP will not be repaid.

We reaffirmed two recommendations from prior material loss reviews related to limits on risky concentrations and documentation of supervisory activity. We did not identify any new recommendations in this material loss review. **(OIG-12-050)**

In-Depth Review of First National Bank of Davis (closed March 11, 2011; estimated loss to the DIF - $25.9 million)

We performed an in-depth review of First National Bank of Davis, Davis, Oklahoma, based on the nature of the bank's unsafe and unsound lending practices.

Due to unsafe or unsound lending practices and violations of law, OCC identified $8.6 million in loan losses that the bank had failed to recognize. OCC noted that the majority of these losses involved extensions of credit to two borrowers. The combination of loans to these borrowers and their related interests totaled almost $12 million, which exceeded the banks legal lending limit of $1.2 million as of December 31, 2010.

Our review of First National Bank of Davis revealed that (1) OCC did not timely identify the extensions of credit that contributed to the bank's failure, (2) OCC's supervisory response to a 2009 federal law enforcement agency investigation of the bank was insufficient, and (3) OCC did not confirm that the bank had addressed previous supervisory directives.

OCC provided responsive corrective action plans to address our recommendations to (1) remind examiners of the importance of (a) performing reconciliations of all reports submitted by bank management to ensure their accuracy and (b) analyzing a bank's new products to determine the effect on credit risk; (2) establish formal guidance to address OCC's response to investigations and requests for information from law enforcement agencies, and (3) remind examiners of the importance of verifying that banks' corrective actions to previously noted deficiencies. **(OIG-12-055)**

Nonmaterial Loss Reviews

During this semiannual reporting period, 8 OCC-regulated financial institutions failed with individual losses below $150 million, the current threshold triggering an MLR. During the period, we issued 9 final audit reports on these nonmaterial reviews (5 on failures during the current period and 4 on failures from the prior period). A list of these audit reports is provided in the Statistical Summary section of this report.

We determined that, for these banks, there were no unusual circumstances surrounding the failures or the supervision exercised by OCC, or the former OTS, that would warrant a more in-depth review of the failures by our office.

Other Banking-Related Work

OCC's Supervision of National Bank's Foreclosure Practices

We performed an audit of OCC's supervision of foreclosure practices at national banks with large mortgage servicing portfolios. We undertook this audit in response to reports of "robo-signing" and document manipulation by financial institutions pursuing foreclosure in connection with the wave of mortgage defaults that took place during the recent economic crisis. Also, this is an area of OCC supervision that we had not previously reviewed.

We found that OCC examination procedures during the period 2008 through 2010 were not sufficient in scope or application to identify significant weaknesses in national banks' foreclosure documentation and processing functions. During the period of our review, OCC did not consider foreclosure documentation and processing to be an area of significant risk and, as a result, did not focus examination resources on this function. The nature and extent of concerns found by OCC during its inter-agency review of mortgage foreclosure processes at major mortgage servicers indicated that OCC underestimated the level of risk in the function during the period we reviewed. We noted a number of conditions in our report that, taken together, may have contributed to this underestimation. In addition, we noted that the *Comptroller's Handbook for Mortgage Banking*, which, among other things, provides the suggested examination procedures covering foreclosures, had not been updated in 13 years.

In responding to our recommendations, OCC stated that it (1) had undertaken a number of actions to enhance examiner focus on operational risk; (2) had reviewed the coding of foreclosure-related consumer complaints and determined that the current coding was sufficient to identify consumer concerns; (3) planned to update the Comptroller's Handbook as part of its broader project to integrate OCC's and the former OTS's policies and examination handbooks; and (4) issued a policy development manual that addresses the development and updating of OCC handbooks. **(OIG-12-054)**

Review of OCC Community Bank Examination and Appeals Processes

We performed an audit to determine for OCC-regulated community banks[5] and federal savings associations (1) examination timelines; (2) how

---

[5] OCC generally defines community banks as those with less than $1 billion in total assets.

OCC ensures consistency in the administration of examinations across the country; (3) the ability of OCC-regulated institutions to question examination results, such as through an Ombudsman, an appeals process, or informal channels; and (4) the frequency and success of such appeals. Our review was requested by the Chairman of the Senate Committee on Banking, Housing, and Urban Affairs. The OIGs of FDIC, FRB, and the National Credit Union Administration were similarly requested to review their respective agencies' processes.

We found that: (1) OCC's four districts established timeliness benchmarks for examinations that were generally consistent, and mostly met; (2) OCC examiners in all districts use the Comptroller's Handbook and the Uniform Financial Institutions Rating System, or "CAMELS," to among other things, promote consistency in the examination process; (3) OCC districts have quality assurance programs to monitor and evaluate the administration of examinations; (4) banks have the ability to question examination results formally and informally through the OCC Ombudsman and the district supervisory offices; and (5) community banks made few appeals.

Our review identified the need for (1) OCC's Western District to expand its quality assurance program to include comprehensive reviews of its examination process; (2) OCC to update and revise its policies and procedures regarding appeals, to include the responsibilities of both the Ombudsman's office and the supervisory district offices, and ensure that guidance provides consistency in interpretation, application, and documentation of the appeals process; and (3) OCC personnel to enter examination data correctly into Examiner View so that OCC can more effectively monitor and measure actual examination timeliness against benchmarks. OCC's corrective actions underway and planned were responsive to our recommendations. **(OIG-12-070)**

Status of the Transfer of OTS Functions

During this semiannual period, our office issued the fourth joint review of the transfer, pursuant to Dodd-Frank, of the functions, employees, funds, and property of the former OTS to the FRB, the FDIC, and OCC. In accordance with Title III of the Act, the transfer occurred in July 2011.

Our joint reviews are also mandated by Dodd-Frank. Our first joint review determined whether the Joint Implementation Plan (Plan) for the transfer prepared by FRB, FDIC, OCC, and OTS conformed to relevant provisions in the Act. After the initial joint review of the Plan, the Act requires that every 6 months we jointly provide a written report on the status of the implementation of the Plan to FRB, FDIC, and OCC, with a copy to Congress. We issued the first and second reports under this requirement in September 2011, and March 2012, respectively.

We concluded in our fourth review that procedures and safeguards are in place as outlined in the Plan to ensure that transferred OTS employees are not unfairly disadvantaged; and that the actions in the Plan that were necessary to transfer the office's property to OCC were implemented. However, we identified certain items are ongoing. For example, OCC was working on a process for certain OTS examiners to acquire the National Bank Examiner commission without taking the full OCC Uniform Commission Examination; a process that would take the examiner's

experience into consideration. Our most recent joint report did not include any recommendations. **(OIG-12-075)**

Recovery Act Audits

During this semiannual period, we issued five audit reports as part of our ongoing oversight of Treasury's more than $20 billion of non-IRS spending authority under the Recovery Act. This includes $3 billion of tax credit authority provided to the CDFI Fund's New Markets Tax Credit program. As part of our continuing oversight responsibilities, we conduct proactive audits of recipients of funds disbursed as part of the Treasury's Recovery Act programs: Payments to States in Lieu of Tax Credits for Low Income Housing (Section 1602), Payments in Lieu of Tax Credits for Specified Energy Properties (Section 1603), and the CDFI Fund New Markets Tax Credit Program. As of September 2012, Treasury has disbursed approximately $20 billion under these programs. We conducted site visits of 45 energy properties valued at approximately $1.5 billion under Treasury's 1603 Program and reviews of 5 state housing authorities are underway comprising more than $1 billion awarded under Treasury's Payments to States in Lieu of Tax Credits for Low Income Housing.

Specified Energy Properties

We audited selected recipients to determine whether the specified energy properties existed, were placed-in-service within the eligible timeframes, and the award amounts were appropriate. During this semiannual period, we issued audit reports on four wind facilities: Panther Creek Wind Farm III (Award amount - $107,636,863), Grand Ridge Energy II LLC (Award amount - $32,300,165), Grand Ridge Energy III LLC (Award amount - $32,094,053);

and Moraine Wind II LLC (Award amount - $28,019,520). We found the subject properties existed and were placed in service within the eligible timeframes. Additionally, the award amounts were appropriate except for $746 of the award amount to Panther Creek Wind Farm III. Treasury management agreed to take appropriate action to seek reimbursement from the recipient. **(OIG-12-062, OIG-12-063, OIG-12-064, and OIG-12-069)**

CDFI Fund Should Revise Policies and Procedures to Clarify Eligibility Reviews Under the New Markets Tax Credit Program

We assessed CDFI Fund's process for reviewing and selecting applicants to receive the additional $3 billion of New Markets Tax Credit authority provided by the Recovery Act for the 2008 and 2009 allocation rounds. We found the Fund timely allocated its additional tax credit authority and noted no exceptions concerning the review and selection of awardees. However, we did identify areas needing improvement with regard to documenting eligibility reviews. While the New Markets Tax Credit program management performed applicant eligibility reviews, they could not support whether additional due diligence reviews were performed on potential affiliates and/or common enterprises identified by the program staff. We also noted instances where the program policies and procedures were not followed. That is, we noted that all documentation related to an applicant's qualified equity investment was not being forwarded to CDFI Fund Legal Counsel for review and that unqualified candidates were not timely notified of their ineligibility to receive a tax credit allocation. These instances, however, did not impact the awarding of 2008 and 2009 tax credit allocations.

We recommended that the New Markets Tax Credit Program policies and procedures be revised to require that all due diligence reviews of applicant's affiliates and/or common enterprises be documented. Furthermore, the program's policies and procedures should be revised to clarify the level of documentation necessary for the performance of legal reviews and the timeliness of notifications to ineligible applicants. CDFI Fund management agreed with our recommendations. **(OIG-12-065)**

Other Performance Audits

FinCEN's BSA IT Modernization Program Is Meeting Milestones, But Oversight Remains Crucial

In November 2006, FinCEN began a system development effort, the BSA IT Mod program, to improve the collection, analysis, and sharing of BSA data. The intent of the system was, among other things, to transition BSA data from IRS to FinCEN. BSA IT Mod is estimated to cost $120 million and is to be completed in 2014.

Pursuant to a Congressional directive, we completed the second in a series of audits of the BSA IT Mod program. The objectives of these audits are to determine if FinCEN is (1) meeting cost, schedule, and performance benchmarks for the program and (2) providing appropriate oversight of contractors. The period covered by our second audit was June 2011 through May 2012.

As of May 2012, we found that BSA IT Mod was on schedule and within budgeted cost. Development of the program met all major scheduled milestones, though the planned completion dates for certain projects were extended. As a noteworthy accomplishment, FinCEN became the authoritative source for BSA data when it transitioned the collection, processing, and storage of all BSA data from IRS in January 2012.

FinCEN tested the performance of BSA IT Mod projects completed as of our review, and resolved many significant issues identified during the testing. To address previously reported concerns with the new system of reports, FinCEN was able to provide BSA data from its E-Filing system in the same format IRS used. That is, it was able to successfully map the data from the new BSA forms to the legacy IRS system format.

Our report also noted the potential risks that still remain to the successful implementation of BSA IT Mod. One potential risk is the interdependency between the component projects. For example, changes made to one project are likely to result in changes to other projects. There is also risk in that additional costs and schedule delays could occur if project resources are reallocated and used to resolve defects, conduct additional testing, or enhance projects during development.

FinCEN did maintain oversight of the BSA IT Mod program. However, we did identify an area of concern where FinCEN discontinued independent program assessments by its Project Management Office. The office turned its focus to providing technical assistance for BSA IT Mod's configuration management after completing two program assessments. While we did not identify any adverse impact to the program so far, as a result of the Program Management Office's reduced independent oversight, we plan to follow up on this area in our upcoming audits of the program. With

respect to Treasury's Office of the Chief Information Officer, we found that the office's monitoring of the program continued, primarily through reviews of FinCEN-prepared documentation.

Our second audit did not make any new recommendations to FinCEN. **(OIG-12-077)**

Treasury's Financial Agent Selection Process for the Agency Mortgage Backed Securities Purchase Program Was Not Fully Documented

HERA authorized the Secretary of the Treasury to purchase obligations and securities issued by the Fannie Mae, Freddie Mac, and the Federal Home Loan Banks. Treasury's authority to make these purchases ended December 31, 2009. The Agency Mortgage Backed Securities (MBS) Purchase Program was one of several programs that Treasury established under its HERA authorities. Under this program, Treasury purchased and sold through financial agents, MBS guaranteed by Fannie Mae and Freddie Mac. These securities are commonly referred to as "agency MBS".[6]

We assessed Treasury's process for (1) determining the services to be carried out by financial agents and (2) selecting and awarding contracts to financial agents. We found that Treasury lacked written policies and procedures for selecting financial agents, and did not fully document its decision-making process. Even so, we found that the approach used for selecting

---

[6] In total, before its purchase authority expired, Treasury acquired $225 billion of agency MBS. Treasury started to sell its agency MBS in March 2011. In March 2012, Treasury announced the completion of its sale of remaining agency MBS and reported that overall, cash returns of $250 billion were received from the agency MBS portfolio through sales, principal, and interest.

financial agents as asset managers for the Agency MBS Purchase Program, as described by Treasury officials, was reasonable. In addition, according to Treasury officials, in the midst of the rapidly developing economic crisis at the time, a deliberate management decision was made to apply resources to other financial stability programs rather than to produce documentation for the financial agent selection process. While we understand the pressures facing the very small group of people involved in the selection process, we believe that a basic tenet of government accountability is maintaining complete and appropriate documentation. Doing so is in the best long-term interest of the Department, should, at a later date, it want to repeat its actions or they be called into question. Accordingly, we recommended that Treasury develop written policies and procedures for selecting financial agents that will, among other things, require timely documentation of the selection process. In a written response, Treasury management generally agreed with the recommendation and stated that they are moving to develop written policies and procedures. **(OIG-12-061)**

FMS Implemented Corrective Actions for Private Collection Agencies

Under the Debt Collection Improvement Act of 1996, FMS maintains a schedule of private collection agencies. These agencies are private sector companies having expertise in the area of debt collection, to assist the government in its debt collection efforts. We reviewed the corrective actions taken by FMS in response to recommendations made in audit reports issued by our office in September 2008 and January 2009 on three private collection agencies. The three agencies were Pioneer Credit Recovery, Inc. (prior OIG report no. OIG-08-043);

Linebarger, Goggan, Blair & Sampson, LLP (prior OIG report no. OIG-08-043); and Diversified Collection Services, Inc. (prior OIG report no. OIG-09-025). We found that FMS has taken steps to ensure the deficiencies found with the private collection agencies in our prior audits were corrected. **(OIG-12-071)**

Information Technology

FMS Successfully Demonstrated Recovery Capability for Treasury Web Application Infrastructure

FMS successfully demonstrated its disaster recovery capability for Treasury Web Application Infrastructure. However, we found that two web applications, Government-Wide Accounting and Shared Accounting Module, did not complete one of the three disaster recovery exercise reconstitution test objectives. Additionally, we found that Treasury Web Application Infrastructure documentation could be improved to include information required by the National Institute of Standards and Technology and the Department. FMS's management response identified corrective actions that met the intent of our two recommendations. **(OIG-12-052)**

Fiscal Year 2012 Audit of Treasury's FISMA Implementation for Intelligence Systems

The Federal Information Security Management Act (FISMA) requires each Inspector General to perform an annual independent evaluation of their agency's information security program and practices. For fiscal year 2012, we determined that Treasury's information security program and practices as they relate to its intelligence systems were adequate, but improvements were needed. Due to the sensitive nature of these systems, our report is classified. **(OIG-12-072)**

Sufficient Protections Were In Place for Departmental Offices' Network and Systems

We performed vulnerability assessments and penetration tests of the Departmental Offices' local area network. We determined that its offices had sufficient protections in place for its local area network. However, we did identify weaknesses that should be remediated to strengthen the security protection for their local area network. Specifically, we found: (1) some local area network devices were configured with insecure default usernames and passwords; (2) a number of local area network servers were missing the latest service packs or running obsolete operating systems; and (3) weaknesses in physical security practices at Treasury buildings, which were quickly addressed after being identified. The Treasury Chief Information Officer agreed with our recommendations and provided responsive corrective action plans. **(OIG-12-078)**

Treasury's Security Management of TNet Needs Improvement

TNet provides Treasury, its bureaus, and on-site contractors with telecommunication services. We concluded that Treasury's security management of TNet needs improvement in that it did not ensure that security controls fully met federal standards and guidelines. Specifically, we found that (1) weaknesses existed in physical security protection of TNet at AT&T's primary Internet Data Center site; (2) not all security controls required by National Institute of Standards and Technology Special Publication 800-53, Revision 3, *Recommended Security Controls for Federal Information Systems and Organizations,* were tested and implemented; (3) TNet's patch management process was not fully implemented; (4) the Contracting Officer's

Representative and TNet Program Management Office did not adequately monitor TNet's security performance measures; (5) Plan of Action and Milestones management could be improved; and (6) certain TNet security procedures were not documented as required. The Treasury Chief Information Officer agreed with our recommendations and provided responsive corrective action plans. **(OIG-12-076)**

Financial Management Audits

We completed three reports described below in support of the audit of Treasury's fiscal year 2012 consolidated financial statements and the financial statement audits of certain other federal agencies.

KPMG LLP (KPMG), under a contract with our office, examined the accounting and procurement processing, and general computer controls related to financial management services provided to various federal agencies by BPD's Administrative Resource Center. The auditor found, in all material respects, that (1) the description of controls for these activities fairly presented the controls that were designed and implemented throughout the period July 1, 2011 to June 30, 2012; (2) these controls were suitably designed; and (3) the controls tested operated effectively throughout the period July 1, 2011 to June 30, 2012. **(OIG-12-068)**

KPMG, under contract with our office, performed examinations that covered (1) the general computer and trust funds management processing controls used for various federal and state agencies' transactions by BPD's Trust Funds Management Branch, and (2) general computer and investment/redemption processing controls used for various federal agencies' transactions by the bureau's Federal Investments Branch. The auditor found, in all material respects, that (1) the description of controls for these activities fairly presented the controls that were designed and implemented throughout the period August 1, 2011 to July 31, 2012; (2) these controls were suitably designed; and (3) the controls tested operated effectively throughout the period August 1, 2011 to July 31, 2012. **(OIG-12-073, OIG-12-074).**

Audits of the fiscal year 2012 financial statements or schedules of the Department and component reporting entities were in progress at the end of this semiannual reporting period. The following table shows audit results for fiscal years 2011 and 2010.

Treasury-audited financial statements and related audits						
	Fiscal year 2011 audit results			Fiscal year 2010 audit results		
Entity	Opinion	Material weak-nesses	Significant deficiencies	Opinion	Material weak-nesses	Significant deficiencies
Government Management Reform Act/Chief Financial Officers Act requirements						
Department of the Treasury	UQ	1	3	UQ	1	3
Internal Revenue Service (A)	UQ	2	1	UQ	2	1
Other required audits						
Department of the Treasury's Special-Purpose Financial Statements	UQ	0	0	UQ	0	0
Office of Financial Stability (TARP) (A)	UQ	0	1	UQ	0	1
Bureau of Engraving and Printing	UQ	0	1	UQ	0	0
Community Development Financial Institutions Fund	UQ	2	0	UQ	0	1
Office of DC Pensions	UQ	0	1	UQ	0	1
Exchange Stabilization Fund	UQ	0	0	UQ	0	1
Federal Financing Bank	UQ	0	0	UQ	0	0
Office of the Comptroller of the Currency	UQ	0	0	UQ	0	0
Office of Thrift Supervision	UQ	0	0	UQ	0	0
Treasury Forfeiture Fund	UQ	0	0	UQ	0	0
Mint						
Financial statements	UQ	0	1	UQ	0	0
Custodial gold and silver reserves	UQ	0	0	UQ	0	0
Other audited accounts that are material to Treasury financial statements						
Bureau of the Public Debt						
Schedule of Federal Debt (A)	UQ	0	0	UQ	0	0
Government trust funds	UQ	0	0	UQ	0	0
Financial Management Service						
Treasury-managed accounts	UQ	0	1	UQ	0	1
Operating cash of the federal government	UQ	0	1	UQ	0	1
Management-initiated audit						
Financial Crimes Enforcement Network	UQ	0	0	UQ	0	0
Alcohol and Tobacco Tax and Trade Bureau	UQ	1	0	UQ	1	0
UQ Unqualified opinion						
(A) Audited by the Government Accountability Office						

The following instances of noncompliance with the Federal Financial Management Improvement Act of 1996, which all relate to IRS, were reported in connection with the audit of the Department's fiscal year 2011 consolidated financial statements. The status of these areas of noncompliance, including progress in implementing remediation plans, will be evaluated as part of the audit of Treasury's fiscal year 2012 financial statements.

Condition	Type of noncompliance
Persistent deficiencies in internal control over unpaid tax assessment systems and information security remain uncorrected. As a result of these deficiencies, IRS was (1) unable to rely upon its systems or compensating and mitigating controls to provide reasonable assurance that its financial statements are fairly presented, (2) unable to ensure the reliability of other financial management information produced by its systems, and (3) at increased risk of compromising confidential IRS and taxpayer information. (first reported in fiscal year 1997)	Federal financial management systems requirements
Automated systems for tax related transactions did not support the net federal taxes receivable amount on the balance sheet and other required supplementary information related to uncollected taxes – compliance assessments and write-offs – as required by Statement of Federal Financial Accounting Standards No. 7, *Accounting for Revenue and Other Financing Sources and Concepts for Reconciling Budgetary and Financial Accounting*. (first reported in fiscal year 1997)	Federal accounting standards

Office of SBLF Program Oversight – Significant Products

State Small Business Credit Initiative

California Needs to Improve Oversight of Programs Participating in the State Small Business Credit Initiative

We determined that most of the $3.6 million spent by California for the SSBCI was used properly. However, $133,250 in loan loss reserves funded under California's Small Business Loan Guarantee Program did not meet requirements. The expenditures constitute a "reckless" misuse of funds, which under the Small Business Jobs Act, Treasury must recoup. California also reported $160,988 in administrative expenses that appeared reasonable but were not supported by proper documentation.

Additionally, 58 percent of the 73 loans we tested lacked borrower and lender assurances and one loan may have gone to a sex offender. In August 2011, we recommended that participating states be required to collect and review assurances and to represent that they are enforcing compliance with all SSBCI program requirements. Treasury agreed to address the collection of assurances from banks, but asserted that banks' reports mandated by the Allocation Agreement between Treasury and participating states serve that purpose. For September and December 2011, California provided Treasury with reports from banks affirming that they complied with lender assurance requirements.

We recommended that Treasury recoup $133,250 identified as a "reckless" misuse of funds; disallow $160,988 in administrative expenses unless California documents actual costs; and consider other actions, including withholding administrative expenses until the State corrects its practices. We also recommended that Treasury determine whether California is in general default of its agreement, and if so, consider suspending or terminating funding to California; and require the State to report on its compliance with borrower/lender assurance requirements and the sex offender status of one borrower. **(OIG-SBLF-12-003)**

Montana's Use of Funds Received from SSBCI

We reported that Montana misused $2.73 million in SSBCI funds on loans for passive real estate investments and the refinancing of prior debt, which are prohibited under the Small Business Jobs Act or SSBCI Policy Guidelines. However, we did not find the misuse to be intentional or reckless, as Montana sought guidance from Treasury before enrolling the loans. Responding to Montana's inquiries, Treasury officials did not provide definitive guidance on the permissibility of passive real estate loans. Treasury may have incorrectly told Montana that refinancing prior debt to the same lender was allowable if the prior debt had matured and new underwriting had occurred. Further, not all of the conversations between Treasury and Montana evidencing the guidance given the State were documented, which would be needed to determine recklessness on the part of the State. Additionally, we determined that $3,426 in personnel costs were not allowable or allocable because the costs were not properly supported.

We recommended that Treasury notify participating states that passive real estate loans and refinancing of prior debt are misuses of funds and encourage them to review their loan enrollments for compliance with SSBCI guidance published on April 25, 2012. We also recommended that Treasury disallow $3,426 in administrative expenses unless Montana can support such costs. Further, we recommended that Treasury establish a procedure to document its responses to state inquiries about permissible uses of funds, and inform states that testimonial evidence will be insufficient in proving that Treasury was consulted about compliance with program requirements. Therefore, States should secure Treasury's written approval before proceeding with loans involving a questionable use of proceeds. Finally, we recommended that Treasury either provide a clear and rigorous legal analysis demonstrating how it concluded that program funds could be used to "re-fund" an existing loan to the same lender, or revise SSBCI Policy and Guidance to disallow such a result. If Treasury continues to allow "re-fundings," it will need to ensure that borrowers are the primary beneficiaries.
(OIG-SBLF-12-006)

Small Business Lending Fund

Soundness of SBLF Investment Decisions Regarding Later-Entry, Withdrawn, and Reconsidered Institutions

We reviewed 47 banks regulated by FDIC and OCC and identified 4 with repayment probabilities below the 80 percent threshold for acceptance into the SBLF program. For 3, compensating factors supported Treasury's approval, but Treasury did not have an adequate basis to approve the fourth. We also found that:

- Regulators' bank examination reports flagged supervisory concerns beyond those disclosed in memos to Treasury. Treasury was aware of these for all but one bank;

- Treasury gave adequate consideration to banks it rejected; and

- Of the 51 banks denied funding, 32 did not meet eligibility requirements. Treasury based denials for the other 19 on the banks' financial health or lending practices.

Because the period of investment for SBLF has passed, we made no recommendations. Treasury had agreed to our previous recommendation to create a watch list for banks with severe financial issues.
(OIG-SBLF-12-004)

Initial SBLF Dividend Rate Calculations Used Incorrect Information

To document SBLF lending gains for purposes of calculating program dividend rates, banks reported their small business lending activity during the baseline period and the program's initial quarter. Our review of these reports determined that 8 of the 10, or 80 percent, of the institutions sampled incorrectly reported qualified lending gains. The banks' errors totaled $74 million, most of which was attributed to one bank over-reporting its baseline by $48 million, or 43 percent. Four of the banks we reviewed overstated their gains, but even larger understatements by 4 other banks caused Treasury to report $45 million less in qualified lending than actually occurred at the eight banks.

The errors observed were largely due to institutions incorrectly transferring information from Call Reports,[7] excluding ineligible loans, or misclassifying loans. As a result, dividend or interest rates, which adjust each quarter, could be incorrect for these institutions. Also due to the bank errors, Treasury's October 26, 2011, *Use of Funds Report* over-reported lending increases for three institutions and under-reported them for four. These errors appeared in two later quarterly reports and will be in subsequent reports unless corrected.

While Treasury will need to test for errors that banks have made in transferring information and excluding loans, it will not be able to identify misclassification errors because it cannot access banks' files and accounting systems. Treasury will also need to follow up with the eight banks, and determine whether they should correct the reports and adjust the initial dividend rates as appropriate. Further, Treasury will need to obtain from two banks support showing that two loans constituted qualified lending. If the institutions cannot produce the documentation, Treasury will need to exclude the loans from small business lending activity reported to Congress. Finally, Treasury will need to ensure that the *October 2012 Use of Funds Report* contains corrections for errors identified in the audit. **(OIG-SBLF-12-005)**

---

[7] Quarterly financial regulatory reports (referred to as Call Reports) vary by type of institution and include Consolidated Reports of Condition and Income, Thrift Financial Reports, Y-9s, Uniform Bank Performance Reports, and Bank Holding Company Performance Reports.

Office of Investigations – Initiatives and Significant Investigations

Initiatives

Improper Payments/Check Forgery Insurance Fund Initiative

As reported in our September 2011 and March 2012 semiannual reports, we embarked upon an initiative aimed at improper payments made by the Treasury Department, specifically improper payments from the Treasury's Check Forgery Insurance Fund. The Fund was established in 1941 to serve as a restitution source to payees when checks drawn upon federal treasury depositories had been lost, forged or stolen.

Since starting this initiative, we have referred 82 subjects for prosecution, with 14 of those subjects being referred during this reporting period. Also during this reporting period, 8 subjects have been charged and arrested. In total, 24 individuals have been convicted and sentenced to date as a result of this initiative.

More recently, we have expanded this initiative to include potentially fraudulent payments made by Treasury using the Automated Clearing House and electronic fund transfer payment systems.

Significant Investigations

Senior BPD Official Investigated for Time and Attendance Abuse

Our office received an allegation that a BPD senior official was committing time and attendance fraud. It also was alleged that the senior official conducted personal business involving a non-profit organization during work hours. The investigation determined that the senior official owed BPD for over 1,200 hours from 2009 to 2012, or approximately $97,800 in salary. The case was declined for prosecution by the U.S. Attorney's Office and was referred to BPD for administrative action in August 2012.

Former Bank President Pleads Guilty to Embezzlement Charge

As a result of a 2-year joint investigation with FDIC OIG and the Federal Bureau of Investigation related to the failure of the First National Bank of Rosedale in Mississippi, the former president of the bank pled guilty to one count of violating 18 U.S.C. 656 – Embezzlement. The former president diverted bank funds to pay personal bills. In addition, by concealing the true identities of the borrowers on several loans and the condition of the loans which led to the bank's failure, his conduct resulted in the subversion of OCC's examination process.

On August 30, 2012, the former bank president was sentenced in U.S. District Court in Aberdeen, Mississippi, to 63 months' imprisonment, a $100 special assessment, and $1,530,000 in restitution.

$4.2 Million Seized in Mutilated Currency Investigation

Our office initiated a joint investigation with the U.S. Secret Service into an allegation that a large national bank sent packages of mutilated currency, on behalf of a state-owned Argentinian bank, totaling approximately $9 million, to the Bureau of Engraving and Printing (BEP) for redemption. BEP determined that the currency submitted was intentionally mutilated in violation of Title 18 U.S.C. 331 - Mutilation, diminution, and falsification of coins/currency.

In May 2012, the U.S. District Court for the District of Columbia issued a seizure warrant which was executed for $4,245,800 in mutilated currency pursuant to Title 18 U.S.C. 1956 – Money Laundering and other civil statutes.

Bond Fraud Investigation Results in Claim for Nearly $75,000

During the reporting period, we concluded an investigation into an allegation that an individual submitted a claim for 114 missing U.S. savings bonds to BPD. As a result of the claim, BPD issued a check to the individual in the amount of $100,950.73. Shortly thereafter, the individual cashed the replacement check and then began cashing-in the purportedly "missing" bonds. The subject admitted to negotiating both the replacement check and 78 of the 114 U.S. savings bonds reported missing. The investigation was declined for prosecution by the U.S. Attorney's Office; however, a collections claim was filed with the U.S. Department of Justice against the individual in the amount of $74,715.50.

Guilty Plea in TreasuryDirect Embezzlement Scheme

The Federal Bureau of Investigation and the Winter Garden Police Department requested OIG's assistance involving an embezzlement scheme in BPD TreasuryDirect accounts. The subject attempted to conceal the embezzlement of funds from a charitable foundation and local businesses by using money from victims to pay other victims, withholding bank statements, and

destroying records. The subject embezzled approximately $1,730,000 from TreasuryDirect accounts and approximately $199,000 from other Orange County, Florida, businesses.

As a result of this investigation, the subject pled guilty to one count of violating 18 U.S.C. 1343 - Wire Fraud, and agreed to make full restitution in the amount of $1,732,315 in U.S. District Court in Orlando, Florida. The subject is awaiting sentencing.

BPD Employee Resigns in Lieu of Termination after Admitting to Viewing Pornography

We initiated an investigation into an allegation that a BPD employee had viewed pornographic images and videos on his government computer during government time. A review and analysis of the employee's government computer found over 800 different pornographic images and numerous pornographic videos. The subject also admitted to viewing the pornographic material on his government computer during his duty hours. After BPD proposed termination, the employee resigned in lieu of termination.

U.S. Mint Employee Suspended for Viewing Pornography at Work

We opened an investigation based on information provided by the U.S. Mint regarding an employee's misuse of a Mint-issued laptop computer to view pornographic sites and images. The investigation included a forensic analysis of the computer and an interview of the employee, both substantiating that the employee used his computer to view pornographic images and sites in violation of Mint policy, and that he had downloaded approximately 1,200 pornographic images on his computer. In August 2012, the findings of the investigation resulted in the suspension of the Mint employee for 30 days.

Individual Arrested for Fraudulent Money Orders

In May 2012, we received information from the Doylestown Township, Pennsylvania, Police Department, alleging that an individual misused the Treasury name and seal to create fraudulent money orders, purportedly paid through Treasury, which were subsequently sent via the U.S. mail to make payments on the subject's personal accounts.

In July 2012, the individual was arrested for violations of Unauthorized Acts in Writing, Theft of Services, and Bad Checks in the Commonwealth of Pennsylvania. Criminal proceedings are ongoing.

Abusive Telephone Caller Sentenced to Probation and Fine

We opened an investigation after receiving information from Treasury Departmental Offices regarding abusive and threatening telephone calls made to a Treasury employee. Our investigation determined the subject made approximately 150 abusive calls to a Treasury employee. Subsequently, the subject was charged with multiple infractions of the Arizona State law.

In April 2012, the subject pled guilty to one charge of Use of Telephone to Annoy or Harass and was sentenced to 11 months' unsupervised probation and a $280 fine, and was ordered to have no contact with Treasury personnel or offices other than IRS.

Two Plead Guilty to Theft and Fraudulent Negotiation of U.S. Treasury Checks

A joint investigation with the U.S. Secret Service was initiated after FMS provided OIG with information that two subjects potentially stole and cashed five U.S. Treasury checks from the mail. In August 2012, the investigation resulted in the two individuals pleading guilty in federal court in Alabama to the theft and fraudulent negotiation of the checks, which had a total combined face value of $6,295. The two individuals face up to 5 years in prison.

Guilty Plea to Charges of False Claims and Fraudulent Negotiation of U.S. Treasury Checks

We initiated an investigation based on information provided by FMS regarding false claims made against the government. The investigation determined that the subject received six U.S. Treasury checks, totaling $8,146, filed claims with FMS claiming he had not received those same checks, and was subsequently issued six replacement checks. The investigation determined that the claims filed by the subject were false.

The investigation led to the subject being charged with two counts of violation of Virginia criminal statute, Obtaining Money by False Pretenses. The subject pled guilty and in April 2012 was sentenced to 7 months' incarceration. The individual was also ordered to make restitution to Treasury.

Following are updates to significant investigative activities reported in prior semiannual reports.

Twelve Arrested in Atlanta and Macon, Georgia, for Theft of Treasury Checks and Tax Refund Fraud

As reported in our September 2011 and March 2012 semiannual reports, an investigation in Atlanta and Macon led to the execution of multiple federal and state search and arrest warrants in which more than 6,000 victims of identity theft were identified along with an estimated $2.3 million in fraud against the government. Since reporting this information, we executed 5 additional search warrants and executed 5 additional arrest warrants on subjects who participated in the theft and negotiation of U.S. Treasury checks. Two subjects have pled guilty and have been sentenced thus far.

Computer Programmer Arrested for Stealing Proprietary Code

As reported in our March 2012 semiannual report, a joint investigation with the Federal Bureau of Investigation resulted in the arrest of a computer programmer for stealing proprietary code from the Federal Reserve Bank of New York. The individual was a contract employee assigned to work on further developing a specific portion of the Government-wide Accounting and Reporting Program software system owned by Treasury.

In May 2012, the individual pled guilty to one count of theft of government property and one count of immigration fraud. The individual faces 10 years in prison and a fine of the greater of $250,000, or twice the gross monetary gain derived from the offense or twice the gross monetary loss to the victims.

Individual Sentenced for Involvement in Tax Refund Scheme Using TreasuryDirect Accounts

As reported in our March 2012 semiannual report, a joint investigation conducted with IRS Criminal Investigations involved an individual who used false tax returns to open BPD TreasuryDirect accounts to purchase U.S. bonds. The subject of the investigation was arrested in December 2010, and was found guilty via jury trial of violation of 18 U.S.C. 1341 – Frauds and Swindles. In April 2012, the subject was sentenced to 10 years' incarceration, and was ordered to pay $1.5 million in restitution.

Mint Police Officer Sentenced for Theft and Tax Evasion

As reported in our September 2011 semiannual report, a Mint police officer pled guilty to theft, mail fraud, money laundering, and tax evasion related to the theft of Presidential $1 coins with missing edge lettering and other items from a Mint facility. The stolen items were subsequently sold to a coin distributor for $2.4 million. In September 2012, the former Mint police officer was sentenced in a New Jersey federal court to serve 36 months of incarceration, followed by 3 years of supervised release. He was also ordered to pay $15,208 in restitution to the Mint and to forfeit $2.3 million in assets. Additionally, he was ordered to resolve a tax liability of $801,651 with IRS.

Other OIG Accomplishments and Activity

OIG Hosts Delegation from Japan

In September 2012, Inspector General Eric Thorson and OIG executives met with a delegation from Japan to discuss the mission of U.S. Government inspectors general and the Treasury OIG. Members of the delegation were Mr. Ryo Kamimura, Deputy Director, Research and International Division, Board of Audit of Japan; and Messrs. Yasuhiro Sakon, Senior Research Analyst, and Sosuke Taguchi, Research Analyst, Public Management and Regional Policy Department, Mitsubishi UFJ Research & Consulting Co., Ltd. Also with the delegation was Ms. Terumi Gale, English-Japanese Interpreter. Treasury's Departmental Offices International Visitors Program facilitated the meeting.

OIG Audit Leadership Roles

Treasury OIG's audit professionals serve on various important public and private professional organizations supporting the federal audit community. Examples of participation in these organizations follow:

Marla Freedman, Assistant Inspector General for Audit, serves as co-chair of the Federal Audit Executive Council's Professional Development Committee which is actively involved in auditor training and development matters. During the period, the Committee undertook a curriculum review of the Introductory Auditor Course offered by the Council of Inspectors General on Integrity and Efficiency (CIGIE) Training Institute. The review is being performed by an interagency

team at the request of the Director of the Institute's Audit, Inspection & Evaluation Academy.

Bob Taylor, Deputy Assistant Inspector General for Performance Audits, and **Kieu Rubb**, Audit Director, are leading a Federal Audit Executive Council project to update the CIGIE Audit Committee's external peer review guide. The update will incorporate changes in the 2011 Revision to *Government Auditing Standards*. A draft of the updated guide was accepted by the CIGIE Audit Committee in September 2012 and is to be presented for final approval by the CIGIE during the next semiannual period. Mr. Taylor and Ms. Rubb also served as facilitators for an August 2012 training course on the external peer review guide sponsored by the National Science Foundation OIG.

Joel Grover, Deputy Assistant Inspector General for Financial Management and Information Technology Audits, serves as co-chair of the Federal Audit Executive Council's Financial Statements Audit Network which develops and coordinates the council's positions on a variety of accounting and auditing issues related to federal financial reporting. Additionally, Mr. Grover served as a co-chair of the Maryland Association of Certified Public Accountants Members in Government Committee.

Jeff Dye, Audit Director, regularly taught modules of the Introductory Auditor Course sponsored by the CIGIE Training Institute.

Senior Special Agent Detailed to Congressional Cybersecurity Staff

An Office of Investigations Senior Special Agent is currently serving on a detail to the

Surveys and Investigations staff of the House of Representatives Committee on Appropriations. Surveys and Investigations personnel perform studies, jointly commissioned by the majority and minority parties, that involve quantitative and qualitative analysis of budgetary, technical, and operational data; meetings and briefings with Executive Branch senior executives and military officers; and briefings to the Committee staff. The Senior Special Agent is supporting classified studies regarding cloud computing and cyber warfare.

The Second Annual Treasury OIG Awards

On May 2, 2012, Treasury OIG held the second annual awards program in the Cash Room of Main Treasury. The program recognized the achievements and outstanding performance of OIG staff during the calendar year 2011. Presented were 12 Individual Achievement Awards, 4 Teamwork Awards, 8 Customer Service Awards to 10 individuals, and 3 Rookie Awards. Also awarded was the Inspector General Leadership Award, the highest honor bestowed to an OIG employee.

Inspector General Eric Thorson presented awards to the following recipients:

Inspector General Leadership Award

Tricia Hollis

Rookie Award

Kathryn Bustell, Andrew Morgan, and Ebonique Poteat

Individual Achievement Award

Susan Barron, John Gauthier, James Howell, Larissa Klimpel, Jason Metrick,

Ken O'Laughlin, John Rizek, Abdil Salah, Loren Sciurba, Sonja Scott, Greg Sullivan, Sharon Torosian

Intra-Component Teamwork Award

SBLF Investment Decision Audit Team
Lisa DeAngelis, Audrey Delaney, and Elizabeth MacDonald

TNET IT Audit Team
Kathy Johnson, Larissa Klimpel, Kevin Mfume, and Abdil Salah

Inter-Component Teamwork Award

SSBCI Definitions Team
Felicia Battista and Rich Delmar

BEP's NexGen $100 Note Security
Theresa Cameron, Deborah Harker, Jerome Marshall, Kieu Rubb, Sonja Scott, and Greg Sullivan

Customer Service Award

Mission Support Branch
Angel Kennon, Nicole Graves, and Sean McCaney

Individual Customer Service Awards
Linda Anderson, Diane Baker, Dawn Buckingham, John Cooper, Nicolas Harrison, Jay Koehler, and Mark Levitt

Statistical Summary

Summary of OIG Activity

For the 6 months ended September 30, 2012

OIG Activity	Number or Dollar Value
Office of Counsel Activity	
Regulation and legislation reviews	3
Instances where information was refused	0
Office of Audit Activities	
Reports issued and other products	33
Disputed audit recommendations	0
Significant revised management decisions	0
Management decision in which the IG disagrees	0
Monetary benefits (audit)	
Questioned costs	$746
Funds put to better use	0
Revenue enhancements	0
Total monetary benefits	$746
Office of Small Business Lending Fund Program Oversight Activities	
Reports issued and other products	4
Disputed audit recommendations	0
Significant revised management decisions	0
Management decision in which the IG disagrees	0
Monetary benefits (audit)	
Questioned costs	$164,414
Funds put to better use	$2,863,250
Revenue enhancements	0
Total monetary benefits	$3,027,664
Office of Investigations Activities	
Criminal and judicial actions (including joint investigations)	
Cases referred for prosecution and/or litigation	61
Cases accepted for prosecution and/or litigation	28
Arrests	12
Indictments/informations	5
Convictions (by trial and plea)	15

Significant Unimplemented Recommendations

For reports issued prior to October 1, 2011

The following list of OIG audit reports with unimplemented recommendations is based on information in Treasury's automated audit recommendation tracking system, which is maintained by Treasury management officials.

Number	Date	Report Title and Recommendation Summary
OIG-06-030	05/06	*Terrorist Financing/Money Laundering: FinCEN Has Taken Steps to Better Analyze Bank Secrecy Act Data but Challenges Remain* FinCEN should enhance the current FinCEN database system or acquire a new system. An improved system should provide for complete and accurate information on the case type, status, resources, and time expended in performing the analysis. This system should also have the proper security controls to maintain integrity of the data. (1 recommendation)
OIG-10-035	2/10	*Management Letter for Fiscal Year 2009 Audit of the Department of the Treasury Financial Statements* The Chief Information Officer, with input from the Office of the Deputy Chief Financial Officer, should implement the use of Secure Sockets Layer for the Treasury Department's Information Executive Repository and CFO Vision applications. (1 recommendation)
OIG-11-036	11/10	*Information Technology: Treasury is Generally in Compliance with Executive Order 13103* The Chief Information Officer should (1) revise Treasury Directive (TD) 85-02 to (a) define authorized software more specifically, (b) require heads of bureaus and offices to ensure that software in their inventory is on the Treasury list of authorized software and remove it if it is not, (c) require the Chief Information Officer to perform periodic audit checks to determine if the bureaus and offices are only using software on the Treasury list of authorized software, and (d) require the bureaus and offices to reconcile their inventory with software license agreements rather than with software purchases; (2) develop procedures to create and manage a list of approved enterprise authorized software; (3) ensure that bureaus remove unauthorized software from Treasury systems; (4) establish and implement department-wide procedures for auditing and tracking software licenses; and

(5) complete deployment of the software management tool.
(5 recommendations)

OIG-11-057   1/11   *The Failed and Costly BSA Direct R&S System Development Effort Provides Important Lessons for FinCEN's BSA Modernization Project*
FinCEN should ensure that adequate contract and financial records are maintained for the current BSA modernization projects to allow for audit as well as accurate reporting to FinCEN management, Treasury's Office of the Chief Information Officer, and the Congress. (1 recommendation)

OIG-11-068   5/11   *Improved Security Over the NexGen $100 Notes Is Necessary*
The Director of the Bureau of Engraving and Printing should evaluate the policy and practices to retain video and digital recordings at the Eastern Currency Facility and the Western Currency Facility in light of the potentially long-term storage needs of the NexGen $100 finished notes and work-in-process sheets.

Summary of Instances Where Information Was Refused

April 1, 2012, through September 30, 2012

In our last semiannual report, we reported that we were being denied the assistance and cooperation of a federal banking regulator in connection with our audit responsibilities. Specifically, FRB had denied us access to information needed for the audit of Treasury's SBLF investment and withdrawal decisions. As part of its mandated oversight responsibilities for the SBLF program, we requested bank examinations from FRB to help it determine whether the regulator had fully disclosed all relevant supervisory information for FRB regulated institutions seeking SBLF funding. The requested information was to be used for an audit ongoing at the time of late-entry institutions into the SBLF program. In response to our initial audit request, and citing 12 C.F.R. § 261.21(d), FRB stated that we had not demonstrated the requisite need for FRB to disclose confidential supervisory information. However, FRB responded to a second request, providing the information we sought, but after the audit had been concluded and a final report was issued. Although our inability to obtain the examination reports timely created a scope limitation for this audit, we determined that the matter has been resolved.

Listing of Audit Products Issued

April 1, 2012, through September 30, 2012

Office of Audit

Financial Audits and Attestation Engagements

Report on the Bureau of the Public Debt Administrative Resource Center's Description of its Financial Management Services and the Suitability of the Design and Operating Effectiveness of its Controls for the Period July 1, 2011 to June 30, 2012, OIG-12-068, 8/17/2012

Report on the Bureau of the Public Debt Federal Investments Branch's Description of its Investment/Redemption Services and the Suitability of the Design and Operating Effectiveness of its Controls for the Period August 1, 2011 to July 31, 2012, OIG-12-073, 9/19/2012

Report on the Bureau of the Public Debt Trust Funds Management Branch's Description of its Trust Funds Management Processing Services and the Suitability of the Design and Operating Effectiveness of its Controls for the Period August 1, 2011 to July 31, 2012, OIG-12-074, 9/19/2012

Information Technology Audits and Evaluations

Information Technology: Financial Management Service Successfully Demonstrated Recovery Capability for Treasury Web Application Infrastructure, OIG-12-052, 5/11/2012

Information Technology: Fiscal Year 2012 Audit of Treasury's FISMA Implementation for Intelligence Systems, OIG-12-072, 9/12/2012, (Classified Report)

Information Technology: Treasury's Security Management of TNet Needs Improvement, OIG-12-076, 9/27/2012

Information Technology: Sufficient Protections Were in Place for Departmental Offices' Network and Systems, OIG-12-078, 9/14/2012

Performance Audits – Material Loss and In-depth Reviews of Failed Banks

Safety and Soundness: Material Loss Review of Integra Bank, National Association, OIG-12-050, 4/12/2012

Safety and Soundness: In-Depth Review of the First National Bank of Davis, Davis, Oklahoma, OIG-12-055, 6/7/2012

Performance Audits – Reviews of Failed Banks Pursuant to Section 987 of the Dodd-Frank Act

Safety and Soundness: Failed Bank Review of Western National Bank, OIG-12-049, 4/5/2012

Safety and Soundness: Failed Bank Review of SCB Bank, OIG-12-051, 5/9/2012

Safety and Soundness: Failed Bank Review of American Eagle Savings Bank, OIG-12-053, 5/24/2012

Safety and Soundness: Failed Bank Review of Home Savings of America, Little Falls, Minnesota, OIG-12-056, 6/18/2012

Safety and Soundness: Failed Bank Review of Fort Lee, Federal Savings Bank, OIG-12-058, 7/12/2012

Safety and Soundness: Failed Bank Review of Charter National Bank and Trust, Hoffman Estates, Illinois, OIG-12-059, 7/20/2012

Safety and Soundness: Failed Bank Review of Plantation Federal Bank, OIG-12-060, 7/26/2012

Safety and Soundness: Failed Bank Review of Security Bank, National Association, North Lauderdale, Florida, OIG-12-066, 8/7/2012

Safety and Soundness: Failed Bank Review of Carolina Federal Savings Bank, Charleston, South Carolina, OIG-12-067, 8/7/2012

Other Performance Audits

Consultation on Solyndra Loan Guarantee Was Rushed, OIG-12-048, 4/3/2012

Safety and Soundness: OCC's Supervision of National Bank's Foreclosure Practices, OIG-12-054, 5/31/2012

Dodd-Frank Act: Treasury Has Made Progress to Stand-up the Office of Financial Research, OIG-12-057, 6/27/2012

Treasury's Financial Agent Selection Process for the Agency Mortgage Backed Securities Purchase Program Was Not Fully Documented, OIG-12-061, 7/31/2012

Recovery Act: Audit of Panther Creek Wind Farm III Payment Under 1603 Program, OIG-12-062, 8/1/2012, **$746 Questioned Cost**

Recovery Act: Audit of Grand Ridge Energy II LLC Payment Under 1603 Program, OIG-12-063, 8/2/2012

Recovery Act: Audit of Grand Ridge Energy III LLC Payment Under 1603 Program, OIG-12-064, 8/2/2012

Recovery Act: The Community Development Financial Institutions Fund Should Revise Policies and Procedures to Clarify Eligibility Reviews Under the New Markets Tax Credit Program, OIG-12-065, 8/3/2012

Recovery Act: Audit of Moraine Wind II LLC Payment Under 1603 Program, OIG-12-069, 8/23/2012

Safety and Soundness: Review of OCC Community Bank Examination and Appeals Processes, OIG-12-070, 8/31/2012

Government-wide Financial Management: The Financial Management Service Implemented Corrective Actions for Private Collection Agencies, OIG-12-071, 9/10/2012

Status of the Transfer of Office of Thrift Supervision Functions, OIG-12-075, 9/26/2012

Terrorist Financing/Money Laundering: FinCEN's BSA IT Modernization Program is Meeting Milestones, But Oversight Remains Crucial, OIG-12-077, 9/27/2012

Other Products

Audit of the Financial Stability Oversight Council's Controls Over Non-public Information, Report to the Financial Stability Oversight Council and the Congress, June 2012, 6/22/2012

Response to Senator Orrin G. Hatch's Inquiries Regarding the Council of Inspectors General on Financial Oversight's Review of the Debt Limit, OIG-CA-12-006, 8/24/2012

Office of SBLF Program Oversight

State Small Business Credit Initiative: California Needs to Improve Its Oversight of Programs Participating in the State Small Business Credit Initiative, OIG-SBLF-12-003, 5/24/2012 **$133,250 Funds Put to Better Use, $160,988 Questioned Cost**

Small Business Lending Fund: Soundness of Investment Decisions Regarding Later-Entry, Withdrawn and Reconsidered Institutions in the SBLF Program, OIG-SBLF-12-004, 7/3/2012

Small Business Lending Fund: Initial Dividend Rate Calculations Used Incorrect Lending Information, OIG-SBLF-12-005, 8/21/2012

State Small Business Credit Initiative: Montana's Use of Funds Received from the State Small Business Credit Initiative, OIG-SBLF-12-006, 9/27/2012 **$2,730,000 Funds Put to Better Use, $3,426 Questioned Cost**

Audit Reports Issued With Questioned Costs

April 1, 2012, through September 30, 2012

Category	Total No. of Reports	Total Questioned Costs	Total Unsupported Costs
For which no management decision had been made by beginning of reporting period	1	$2,080,452	0
Which were issued during the reporting period	3	$165,160	0
Subtotals	4	$2,245,612	0
For which a management decision was made during the reporting period	1	$2,080,452	0
Dollar value of disallowed costs	1	$284,827	0
Dollar value of costs not disallowed	1	$1,795,625	0
For which no management decision was made by the end of the reporting period	3	$165,160	0
For which no management decision was made within 6 months of issuance	0	0	0

Audit Reports Issued With Recommendations That Funds Be Put to Better Use

April 1, 2012, through September 30, 2012

Category	Total No. of Reports	Total	Savings	Revenue Enhancement
For which no management decision had been made by beginning of reporting period	0	0	0	0
Which were issued during the reporting period	2	$2,863,250	$2,863,250	0
Subtotals	2	$2,863,250	$2,863,250	0
For which a management decision was made during the reporting period	0	0	0	0
Dollar value of recommendations agreed to by management	0	0	0	0
Dollar value based on proposed management action	0	0	0	0
Dollar value based on proposed legislative action	0	0	0	0
Dollar value of recommendations not agreed to by management	0	0	0	0
For which no management decision was made by the end of the reporting period	2	$2,863,250	$2,863,250	0
For which no management decision was made within 6 months of issuance	0	0	0	0
A recommendation that funds be put to better use denotes funds could be used more efficiently if management took actions to implement and complete the recommendation including: (1) reduction in outlays, (2) de-obligations of funds from programs or operations, (3) costs not incurred by implementing recommended improvements related to operations, (4) avoidance of unnecessary expenditures noted in pre-award review of contract agreements, (5) any other savings which are specifically identified, or (6) enhancements to revenues of the federal government..				

Previously Issued Audit Reports Pending Management Decisions (Over 6 Months)

There are no previously issued audit reports pending management decisions for the reporting period.

Significant Revised Management Decisions

April 1, 2012, through September 30, 2012

There were no significant revised management decisions during the period.

Significant Disagreed Management Decisions

April 1, 2012, through September 30, 2012

There were no management decisions this period with which the IG was in disagreement.

Peer Reviews

April 1, 2012, through September 30, 2012

Office of Audit and Office of SBLF Program Oversight

Audit organizations that perform audits and attestation engagements of federal government programs and operations are required by *Government Auditing Standards* to undergo an external peer review every 3 years. The objectives of an external peer review are to determine, during the period under review, whether, the audit organization's system of quality control was suitably designed and whether the audit organization was complying with its quality control system in order to provide the audit organization with reasonable assurance that it was conforming to applicable professional standards.

During this semiannual period, the U.S. Agency for International Development OIG conducted an external peer review of Treasury OIG's Office of Audit and Office of SBLF Program Oversight that covered year ended March 31, 2012. Treasury OIG received a *"pass"* rating. The external peer review did not identify any recommendations. The peer review report may be viewed on the Treasury OIG website at

http://www.treasury.gov/about/organizational-structure/ig/Audit%20Reports%20and%20Testimonies/TOIG%20Peer%20Review.pdf

At the end of the semiannual period, we were conducting an external peer review of the Department of Education OIG's audit organization.

Office of Investigations

CIGIE mandates that the investigative law enforcement operations of all OIGs undergo peer reviews every 3 years in order to ensure compliance with (1) the council's investigations quality standards and with (2) the relevant guidelines established by the Office of the Attorney General for the United States.

Our Office of Investigations was not the subject of a CIGIE peer review during this reporting period. However, during this period, our OIG conducted a CIGIE peer review of the investigative operations at the Department of Transportation's (DOT) OIG. The final report was released in September and we reported that the system of internal safeguards and management procedures for DOT OIG's investigative functions were in compliance with quality standards established by CIGIE and Attorney General Guidelines. These safeguards and procedures provide reasonable assurance that DOT OIG conforms to professional standards in the conduct of its investigations.

Bank Failures and Nonmaterial Loss Reviews

We conducted reviews of 7 failed banks supervised by OCC with losses to the DIF that did not meet the definition of a material loss in FDIA. These reviews were performed to fulfill the requirements found in 12 U.S.C. § 1831o(k). The term "material" loss which, in turn, triggers an MLR be performed is, for 2012 and 2013, a loss to the DIF that exceeds $150 million; and, for 2014 going forward, a loss to the DIF that exceeds $50 million (with provisions to increase that trigger to a loss that exceeds $75 million under certain circumstances).

For losses that are not material, FDIA requires that each 6-month period, the OIG of the federal banking agency must (1) identify the estimated losses that have been incurred by the DIF during that 6-month period and (2) determine the grounds identified by the failed institution's regulator for appointing the FDIC as receiver, and whether any unusual circumstances exist that might warrant an in-depth review of the loss. For each 6-month period, we are also required to prepare a report to the failed institutions' regulator and the Congress that identifies (1) any loss that warrants an in-depth review, together with the reasons why such a review is warranted and when the review will be completed; and (2) any losses where we determine no in-depth review is warranted, together with an explanation of how we came to that determination. The table below fulfills this reporting requirement to the Congress for the 6-month period ended September 30, 2012. We issue separate audit reports on each review to OCC.

Bank Failures and Non Material Loss Reviews

Bank Name/Location	Date Closed/ Loss to the DIF	OIG Summary of Regulator's Grounds for Receivership	In-Depth Review Determination	Reason/ Anticipated Completion Date of the In-Depth Review
Fort Lee Federal Savings Bank Fort Lee, New Jersey	April 20, 2012 $14 million	• Dissipation of assets or earnings due to unsafe and unsound practices • Capital impaired • Failed to submit acceptable capital restoration plan	No	No unusual circumstances noted
Plantation Federal Bank Pawleys Island, South Carolina	April 27, 2012 $76 million	• Dissipation of assets or earnings due to unsafe and unsound practices • Capital impaired	No	No unusual circumstances noted
Inter Savings Bank, FSB Maple Grove, Minnesota	April 27, 2012 $119.2 million	• Dissipation of assets or earnings due to unsafe and unsound practices • Capital impaired	No	No unusual circumstances noted
Palm Desert National Bank Palm Desert, California	April 27, 2012 $23.4 million	• Dissipation of assets or earnings due to unsafe and unsound practices • Capital impaired • Unsafe and unsound practices were likely to seriously prejudice the interests of the DIF	No	No unusual circumstances noted
Security Bank North Fort Lauderdale, Florida	May 4, 2012 $13.7 million	• Dissipation of assets or earnings due to unsafe and unsound practices • Capital impaired	No	No unusual circumstances noted

Bank Failures and Non Material Loss Reviews				
Bank Name/Location	Date Closed/ Loss to the DIF	OIG Summary of Regulator's Grounds for Receivership	In-Depth Review Determination	Reason/ Anticipated Completion Date of the In-Depth Review
Alabama Trust Bank Sylacauga, Alabama	May 18, 2012 $11.4 million	• Dissipation of assets or earnings due to unsafe and unsound practices • Capital impaired	No	No unusual circumstances noted. However, our review revealed certain questionable activity by Alabama Trust Bank management that was referred by our auditors to the OIG Office of Investigations.
Carolina Federal Savings Bank Charleston, South Carolina	June 8, 2012 $17.1 million	• Dissipation of assets or earnings due to unsafe and unsound practices • Capital impaired • Failed to submit acceptable capital restoration plan	No	No unusual circumstances noted
Second Federal Savings & Loan Association of Chicago Chicago, Illinois	July 22, 2012 $76.9 million	• Dissipation of assets or earnings due to unsafe and unsound practices • Capital impaired • Failed to submit acceptable capital restoration plan	Yes	Unusual circumstances identified; estimated completion date is September 2013

References to the Inspector General Act

	Requirement	Page
Section 4(a)(2)	Review of legislation and regulations	31
Section 5(a)(1)	Significant problems, abuses, and deficiencies	7-28
Section 5(a)(2)	Recommendations with respect to significant problems, abuses, and deficiencies	7-28
Section 5(a)(3)	Significant unimplemented recommendations described in previous semiannual reports	32-33
Section 5(a)(4)	Matters referred to prosecutive authorities	31
Section 5(a)(5)	Summary of instances where information was refused	33
Section 5(a)(6)	List of audit reports	34-36
Section 5(a)(7)	Summary of significant reports	7-28
Section 5(a)(8)	Audit reports with questioned costs	37
Section 5(a)(9)	Recommendations that funds be put to better use	37
Section 5(a)(10)	Summary of audit reports issued before the beginning of the reporting period for which no management decision had been made	38
Section 5(a)(11)	Significant revised management decisions made during the reporting period	38
Section 5(a)(12)	Management decisions with which the IG is in disagreement	38
Section 5(a)(13)	Instances of unresolved FFMIA noncompliance	21
Section 5(a)(14)	Results of peer reviews conducted of Treasury OIG by another OIG	38-39
Section 5(a)(15)	List of outstanding recommendations from peer reviews	38-39
Section 5(a)(16)	List of peer reviews conducted by Treasury OIG, including a list of outstanding recommendations from those peer reviews	38-39
Section 5(d)	Serious or flagrant problems, abuses, or deficiencies	N/A
Section 6(b)(2)	Report to Secretary when information or assistance is unreasonably refused	33

Abbreviations

BEP	Bureau of Engraving and Printing
BPD	Bureau of the Public Debt
BSA	Bank Secrecy Act
BSA IT Mod	BSA IT Modernization
CDFI	Community Development Financial Institutions
CIGFO	Council of Inspectors General on Financial Oversight
CIGIE	Council of the Inspectors General on Integrity and Efficiency
DIF	Deposit Insurance Fund
Dodd-Frank	Dodd-Frank Wall Street Reform and Consumer Protection Act
DOE	Department of Energy
EESA	Emergency Economic Stabilization Act
Fannie Mae	Federal National Mortgage Association
FDIA	Federal Deposit Insurance Act
FDIC	Federal Deposit Insurance Corporation
FIO	Federal Insurance Office
FinCEN	Financial Crimes Enforcement Network
FISMA	Federal Information Security Management Act
FMS	Financial Management Service
FRB	Board of Governors of the Federal Reserve System
Freddie Mac	Federal Home Loan Mortgage Corporation
FSOC	Financial Stability Oversight Council
HERA	Housing and Economic Recovery Act
IRS	Internal Revenue Service
IT	information technology
KPMG	KPMG LLP
MLR	material loss review
MBS	mortgage backed securities
OCC	Office of the Comptroller of the Currency
OFAC	Office of Foreign Assets Control
OFR	Office of Financial Research
OIG	Office of Inspector General
OTS	Office of Thrift Supervision
Plan	Joint Implementation Plan
Recovery Act	American Recovery and Reinvestment Act of 2009
SBLF	Small Business Lending Fund
Solyndra	Solyndra, LLC
SSBCI	State Small Business Credit Initiative
TARP	Troubled Asset Relief Program
TNet	Treasury Network

Statue of Alexander Hamilton, 1st Secretary of the Treasury (1789 to 1795)
South side of the Treasury Building in Washington, D.C.

contact us

Office of Inspector General
1500 Pennsylvania Avenue, N.W.
Room 4436
Washington, D.C. 20220
Phone: (202) 622-1090;
Fax: (202) 622-2151

Office of Small Business Lending
Fund Program Oversight
1425 New York Avenue, Suite 5041
Washington, D.C. 20220
Phone: (202) 622-1090;
Fax: (202) 927-5421

Office of Audit
740 15th Street, N.W., Suite 600
Washington, D.C. 20220
Phone: (202) 927-5400;
Fax: (202) 927-5379

Office of Investigations
1425 New York Avenue, Suite 5041
Washington, D.C. 20220
Phone: (202) 927-5260;
Fax: (202) 927-5421

Office of Counsel
740 15th Street, N.W., Suite 510
Washington, D.C. 20220
Phone: (202) 927-0650;
Fax: (202) 927-5418

Office of Management
740 15th Street, N.W., Suite 510
Washington, D.C. 20220
Phone: (202) 927-5200;
Fax: (202) 927-6492

Boston Audit Office
408 Atlantic Avenue, Room 330
Boston, Massachusetts 02110-3350
Phone: (617) 223-8640;
Fax: (617) 223-8651

Treasury OIG Hotline
Call Toll Free: 1.800.359.3898

Treasury OIG Web Page

OIG reports and other information are now available via the Internet. The address is
http://www.treasury.gov/about/organizational-structure/ig/Pages/default.aspx

www.ingramcontent.com/pod-product-compliance
Lightning Source LLC
Chambersburg PA
CBHW052015280526
45793CB00005B/995